Poems and Prayers for Grieving Parents

Julie Posey

Copyright 2012 Julie Posey All Rights Reserved

This book contains material protected under International and Federal Copyright Laws and Treaties. Any unauthorized reprint or use of this material is prohibited. No part of this book may be reproduced or transmitted in any form or by any means, electronic or mechanical, including photocopying, recording, or by any information storage and retrieval system without express written permission from the author.

japosey64@gmail.com

ISBN-13: 978-1475006742
ISBN-10: 1475006748

To K.P, C.P, and D.C. who I'll always remember.

Contents

Contents 9
Preface 9
A Butterfly on a Child's Grave 13
A Child Loaned 14
A Remedy 16
A Little Child 17
A Lock of Hair 18
A Prodigal Son 19
A Mother's Grief 20
A Mother's Lament for the Death of Her Son 22
A Mother's Only Daughter 23
Bereaved Parents Comforted 24
Blessed Are They That Mourn 26
Better to Hope 27
Do Not Stand At My Grave and Weep 27
A Prayer for Family Comfort 29
A Prayer for the Missing 29
Consolation in Sorrow 30
Forget Me Not 31
God's Care 31
The Lost Child 32
First Spring Violet 33
Faded Lavender 34
I Gave My Boy to His Country 36
The Day God Took You Home 37
It Is Not For Thee I Am Weeping 38
Why Do You Weep? 41

Lines to a Young Mother 42
In My Despair I Sit.. 43
Mother, What Is Death? 44
Pearls of Beauty 46
She Died in Beauty 46
Tears 48
The Comfort of the Promises 49
The Bottom Drawer 50
The Death of Infants 52
The Last Kiss 54
The Star and the Child 56
The Tear of Sympathy 57
Thinking 58
Weep Not For Her 59
To a Bereaved Mother 60
We Will Laugh Again 62
To an Infant in Heaven 63
To Each His Own 65
To a Friend on the Loss of a Child 66
Psalms of Comfort 68

Preface

There comes a time in nearly everyone's life when they suddenly become acquainted with grief. During these trying times, we are likely to experience a variety of emotions caused by the most intense physical or emotional pain we have ever felt.

This book is composed of poetic writings and other works from authors of the past whose sorrows were softened with sympathy. There are also verses from the Holy Bible that speak words of consolation and hope to those who are mourning.

It is my hope that mothers and fathers will be able to see through their tears and recognize a resemblance of their own cherished loved one as they turn the pages of this book.

A Butterfly on a Child's Grave

A butterfly basked on an infant's grave,
Where a lily had ventured to grow.
Why are you here with your blaring dye,
Where she of the bright and the sparkling eye
Must sleep in the graveyard low?

Then it lightly soared through the sunny air,
And spoke from its shining track:
"I was a worm till I won my wings,
And she for whom you mourn,
like a seraph sings.
Would you call the blessed one back?"

A Child Loaned

I'll lend you for a little time
"A child of Mine," He said,
"For you to love the while she lives,
And mourn for when she's dead.

It may be six or seven years
Or twenty-two or three,
But will you, till I call her back,
Take care of her for Me?

She'll bring her charms to gladden you,
and should her stay be brief,
You'll have her lovely memories
As solace for your grief.

I cannot promise she will stay,
Since all from earth return,
But there are lessons taught down there
I want this child to learn.

I've looked this wide world over
In my search for teachers true,
And from the throngs that crowd life's
lanes, I have selected you.

"Now will you give her all your love,
Not think the labor vain,
Nor hate Me when I come to call
And take her back again?"

I enjoyed hearing them say,
"Dear Lord, Your will be done,
For all the joy your child shall bring,
The risk of grief we'll run."

We'll shelter her with tenderness,
We'll love her while we may,
And for the happiness we've known,
Forever grateful stay.

But should the angels call for her
Much sooner than we planned,
We'll brave the bitter grief that comes
And try to understand.

*In my distress I called upon the LORD, and cried
unto my God: he heard my voice out of his temple,
and my cry came before him, even into his ears.
Psalm 18:6*

A Remedy

For every evil under the sun,
There is a remedy, or there is none.
If there is one, try to find it.
If there is none, never mind it.

*In my distress I called upon the LORD, and cried
unto my God: he heard my voice out of his temple,
and my cry came before him, even into his ears.
Psalm 18:6*

A Little Child

There's nothing more pure in heaven,
And nothing on earth more mild,
More full of light that is all divine,
Than the smile of a little child.

The sinless lips half parted,
With breath as sweet as the air,
And the light that seems so glad to shine,
In the gold of the sunny hair.

I feel that the gates of heaven
Are nearer than I knew,
That the light and the hope of that sweeter world,
Like the dawn, are breaking through.

*He healeth the broken in heart,
and bindeth up their wounds.
Psalm 147:3*

A Lock of Hair

Few things in this weary world are so delightful as keepsakes. Nor do they ever, to my heart at least, nor to my eye, lose their tender, their powerful charm! How slight, how small, how a tiny memorial saves a beloved one from oblivion.

Worn on the finger, or in a locket close to the heart, especially if they be dead. No thought is so insupportable as entire, total, blank forgetfulness, when the creature that once laughed, sang and wept with us, close to our side, in our arms, is as if her smiles, her voice, her tears, her kisses, had never been felt. She and her memories all swallowed up in the nothingness of the dust.

Of all keepsakes, memorials, relics, most dearly, most precious, do I love a little lock of hair. When on the head it was so beautiful. How spiritual the undying glossiness seems. As if to be a sad memento. Everything else gone to nothing except that soft, smooth, burnished, and glorious fragment of the adornment that once hung in clouds and glowed like sunshine over an angel's brow.

Oh, a lock of hair is far more valuable than any photo. It is part of the beloved person herself and it belongs to the ringlets that often, long ago, may have been scattered, like a shower of sunbeams, over your shoulders. But now, solemn thoughts sadden the beauty once so bright and so radiant. The longer you gaze on it, the more and more it seems to speak back to you, "Are you weeping for me?"

Indeed, a tear, true to the imperishable affections in which all nature seemed to rejoice, bears witness that the person we loved so much, is never forgotten. She has been dead for so many long, weary days, months, and years, but not forgotten during an hour of absence, that came like a passing cloud between us and the sunshine of our living in her loving smiles.

Thou shalt increase my greatness, and comfort me on every side.
Psalm 71:21

A Prodigal Son

Does that lamp still burn in my Father's house,
Which he kindled the night I went away?
I turned once beneath the cedar boughs,
and marked it gleam with a golden ray;
Did he think to light me home some day?

Hungry here with the crunching swine,
Hungry harvest have I to reap;
In a dream I count my Father's kine,
I hear the tinkling bells of his sheep,
I watch his lambs that browse and leap.

There is plenty of bread at home,
His servants have bread enough and to spare;
The purple wine-fat froths with foam,
Oil and spices make sweet the air,
While I perish hungry and bare.

Rich and blessed those servants,
rather than I who see not my Father's face!
I will arise and go to my Father:-
"Fallen from sonship, beggared of grace,
grant me, Father, a servant's place."

My soul melteth for heaviness: strengthen
thou me according unto thy word.
Psalm 119:28

Julie Posey

A Mother's Grief

To mark the sufferings of the babe,
That cannot speak its woe.
To see the infant tears gush forth,
Yet know not why they flow.

To meet the meek uplifted eye,
That fain would ask relief.
Yet cannot tell the agony,
This is a mother's grief.

To watch the last dreaded strife draw near.
And pray that struggle be brief,
Though all is ended with its fear-
This is a mother's grief!

To see, in one short hour, decayed
The hope of future years,
To feel how vain a father's prayers,
How vain a mother's tears.

To think the cold grave now must close
Over what was once the chief
Of all the treasured joys of earth-
This is a mother's grief!

Yet when the first wild throb is past
Of anguish and despair,

To lift the eye of faith to heaven,
And think, "My little child is there."

The best can dry the gushing tears,
This yields the heart relief
Until the Christian's pious hope
Overcomes a mother's grief.

Yet when the first wild throb is past
Of anguish and despair,
To lift the eye of faith to heaven,
And think, "My child is there."

This best can dry the gushing tears,
This yields the heart relief;
Until the Christian's pious hope
Overcomes a mother's grief.

For our light affliction, which is but for a moment, worketh
for us a far more exceeding and eternal weight of glory;
While we look not at the things which are seen, but at the things
which are not seen: for the things which are seen are temporal;
but the things which are not seen are eternal.
2 Corinthians 4:17-18

Julie Posey

A Mother's Lament for the Death of Her Son

Fate gave the word, the arrow sped,
And pierced my darling's heart.
And with him all the joys are fled
Life can to me impart.

By cruel hands the sapling drops,
In dust dishonored laid.
So fell the pride of all my hopes,
My age's future shade.

The mother finch in the brake,
Bewails her ravished young.
So I, for my lost darling's sake,
Lament the live day long.

Death, often I've feared your fatal blow.
Now, fond, I bare my chest.
Oh, do you kindly lay me low
With him I love, at rest.

Humble yourselves therefore under the mighty hand of God, that he may exalt you in due time: Casting all your care upon him; for he careth for you.
1 Peter 5:6-7

A Mother's Only Daughter

A mother had a lovely child,
A little girl of seven.
She loved her with a love so wild,
She'd not have parted with that child
For all the wealth of Heaven.

Her sole, supremest, dearest joy
Was centered in that creature.
She loved her better than her boy,
And thought that Death would never destroy
One portion of her feature.

But we are weak, and God is strong.
The tyrant, death, soon sought her.
He snatched the one she'd cherished long,
The one she'd loved too deep, too strong.

Bereft her of her daughter,
They laid her in her last low bed,
And not a word was spoken
But we have often heard it said,
The mother glanced once on the dead,
And then her heart was broken.

The LORD is nigh unto them that are of a broken heart; and saveth such as be of a contrite spirit.
Psalm 34:18

Bereaved Parents Comforted

Bereaved parents do not cling to feelings of hopelessness when your children are taken from you in death. Consider that Jesus is only saying to you in another form what He said to His disciples long ago, "Suffer the little children to come unto me and forbid them not: for of such is the kingdom of God."

A child's death may just be their going to Him, for I have no doubt whatsoever of the salvation of infants. It is not indeed a doctrine distinctly revealed but it may, I think, be inferred from many passages of scripture, and from the whole character of the gospel itself.

The very words which I have quoted, even if there were no others, warrant the conclusion that infants are received into that kingdom of God which stretches into eternity and if this be so, would you want to be like Rachel, "refusing to be comforted?"

Consider to whom the child has gone. He or she has been taken to the arms of Jesus, and to the bright glory of the heaven. Nothing now can blur their happiness, or dim the luster of their joy, or dampen the spirit of their song. If the child could speak to you, from their abode of bliss, they would say to you, "Don't weep for me but weep for yourselves because you are not able to see the happiness I am seeing."

Also consider from what the child has been taken. The little one has been safely removed from earth, with its pains and hardships, and its sufferings and sorrows. Look back upon your own past, and tell me if you can imagine, without a feeling of grief, the idea of your children passing through such trials as those which have met you in the world? Would you wish that their hearts should be broken as yours have been, by the harshness of an unfeeling world, or by the ingratitude of those whom you have served?

No, in view of the agony of this very bereavement, would you wish that a similar sorrow should be on any child? And yet does not their continuance in the world involve in it the endurance of all these things? In some ways, would it be a matter of thankfulness that the child has reached heaven without having to pass through the full bitterness of earth?

Above all, can you contemplate the spiritual dangers with which the world's environment, and not feel grateful that your little ones are now eternally safe from them? Think of the temptations that you may have encountered, and of the dreadful battles which you fought with them, and how near you were to being conquered by them. Now, let me ask if in this view you can feel other than gladness since they have gained the victory without the perils and hardships of the fight?

Perhaps, had they been exposed to these dangers they would have fallen before them. Perhaps, had they lived they would have grown up only to fill your hearts with sadness, and "to bring your gray hairs with sorrow to the grave;" but all this is now impossible, for they are safe with Jesus.

This is certainly not meant to minimize your pain or to dismiss it as if it were nothing. It is so very hard to part with a young child. In fact, the death of a child is probably the most difficult types of adversity that could ever occur.

Grieving parents, think about these things, while you mourn and then over time, your bereavement will seem to be, as it in reality is, a token of love and not of anger from the Lord above.

> *"Oh, not in cruelty, not in wrath,*
> *The Reaper came that day;*
> *'Twas an angel visited the green earth,*
> *And took the flowers away."*

Julie Posey

Blessed Are They That Mourn

Oh, deem not they are blessed alone
Whose lives a peaceful tenor keep.
The power who pities man, has shown
A blessing for the eyes that weep.

The light of smiles shall fill again
The lids that overflow with tears,
And weary hours of woe and pain
Are promises of happier years.

There is a day of sunny rest
For every dark and troubled night
And grief may bide an evening guest,
But joy shall come with early light.

And thou, who over thy friend's low bier
Does shed the bitter drops like rain,
Hope that a brighter, happier sphere
Will give him to thy arms again.

Nor let the good man's trust depart,
Though life its common gifts deny,
Though with a pierced and bleeding heart,
And spurned of men he goes to die.

For God hath marked each sorrowing day
And numbered every secret tear,
And heaven's long age of bliss shall pay
For all His children suffer here.

Blessed are they that mourn: for they shall be comforted.
Matthew 5:4

Better to Hope

Better to hope, though the clouds hang low.
And to keep the eyes still lifted,
For the sweet blue sky will soon peep through
When the ominous clouds have drifted!

There was never a night without a day,
Or an evening without a morning
And the darkest hour, as the proverb goes,
Is just before the dawning.

Do Not Stand At My Grave and Weep

Do not stand at my grave and weep
I am not there, I do not sleep.
I am a thousand winds that blow,
I am the diamond glints on snow,
I am the sun on ripened grain,
I am the gentle autumn rain.

When you awaken in the morning's hush,
I am the swift uplifting rush
Of quiet birds in circled flight.
I am the soft stars that shine at night.
Do not stand at my grave and cry,
I am not there, I did not die.

When I would comfort myself against sorrow, my heart is faint in me.
Jeremiah 8:18

A Prayer for Family Comfort

Oh God, our Father, we your children bow humbly at your feet in our time of sorrow. To whom can we go but to you? We desire to submit ourselves to your will. You have laid your hand upon us and our broken hearts. But in our grief we will put our trust in you. Even so, Lord, you have a purpose for this tragedy.

We thank you for the comforts that come to us from the gospel, for the words of divine promise which whisper themselves into our hearts, for the assurance of the sympathy of Christ, who also wept with His friends in their bereavement.

We now ask that you quiet our hearts and comfort us with your peace. May the memories of the vanished life stay in our hearts as holy benedictions. May our lives be all the sweeter for the grief that has touched them. We pray for the blessings of your love, we ask this in the name of Christ. Amen.

A Prayer for the Missing

Oh God, You are present everywhere. Your eyes keep watch over all places at all times. We commend to your loving thought and care our absent loved ones, praying that your will keep them from evil and bless them in the experiences through which they are passing. Preserve them from accident, from moral harm, from sickness, from sin. Bring them back to us in due season, enriched for better life and greater usefulness. We ask in Jesus Christ our Lord. Amen.

But they that wait upon the LORD shall renew their strength
they shall mount up with wings as eagles; they shall run,
and not be weary; and they shall walk, and not faint.
Isaiah 40:3

Julie Posey

Consolation in Sorrow

It is not to the tomb that God will carry those whom you love. The fleshly garments may be carried there, but the living soul God places not in the tomb. Think, then, that at any moment the objects of your fond love may be withdrawn to the spiritual world. Thus your affection will be spiritualized.

You will regard those whom God kindly makes dear, not as beings of time, but as immortal beings. Your love will be love of the soul. You will become true friends to one another, as angels are friends to one another in heaven.

You will find mutual delight in prayer, and in efforts to aid each other along life's pilgrimage. Every day you will gather a leaf from the tree of Life, and weave it into the band which unites you to the beloved one. When at last the hour of separation comes, you will find that the band of union has become altogether amaranthine, and not a leaf shall wither before death's cold breath.

Affections, thus spiritualized, thus rendered immortal, what beauty and happiness do they impart to life! what superiority do they give over death! And when the hour of reunion comes to those who have thus loved, Oh, its bliss, what tongue can tell? That bliss may the heavenly Father graciously grant unto us all!

*Though I walk in the midst of trouble, thou
wilt revive me: thou shalt stretch forth thine hand against
the wrath of mine enemies, and thy right hand shall save me.
Psalm 138:*

Forget Me Not

My little one,
You have left us too soon.
Though my body can no longer hold you,
I hold you forever in my heart.
As precious and beautiful as this flower caught in time a mother's love does not forget.

God's Care

I fear not, my Father, the tempest's loud roar,
Nor dread the huge breakers on the rock girded shore.
Thy presence is with me, my refuge is near,
With help all sufficient, oh, why should I fear?
Though billows of sorrow should roll over my head,
My sun sink in darkness, and joys be all dead,
Thy presence will cheer me, and specters will flee,
For who can upset me while trusting in thee?

*For I reckon that the sufferings of this present
time are not worthy to be compared with
the glory which shall be revealed in us.
Romans 8:1*

Julie Posey

The Lost Child

You, who have hid forever from these eyes,
You, who hast laid so long in that dark sleep,
Unconscious that your mother yet does weep
Beside your early tomb with heavy sighs.

My own fair child, your voice no more replies
To my accustomed call of her whose tone
Dies on the chilly wind, unheard, unknown.
If your young spirit, bending from the skies,

Can view the wretched in the hour of prayer,
Look on me now, and though it may not be
That I shall trace your heavenly form in air,
Shadow immortal, that I cannot see,
O wander round, and I shall deem I hear
Your low voice whisper, "Weep no more for me."

*Be of good courage, and he shall strengthen
your heart, all ye that hope in the LORD.
Psalm 31:24*

First Spring Violet

Spring has come, dear father!
I've a violet found,
Growing in its beauty
From the cold, dark ground.

You are sad, dear father,
Tears are in your eye,
You're not glad to see it.
Father, tell me why?

Then you told me, father,
That the flowers would fade,
And their withered blossoms
On the earth be laid.

But you said, as springtime
Their buds would restore,
Baby boy is in heaven
To live forevermore.

Weep no more, dear father!
Violets are in bloom,
And your darling baby
Lives beyond the tomb.

He that goeth forth and weepeth, bearing precious seed, shall doubtless come again with rejoicing, bringing his sheaves with him.
Psalm 126:6

Julie Posey

Faded Lavender

How prone we are to hide and hoard
Each little treasure time has stored,
To tell of happy hours!
We lay aside with tender care
A tattered book, a lock of hair,
A bunch of faded flowers.

When death has led with silent hand
Our darlings to the "Silent Land,"
While we sit bereft.
But time goes on and we rise,
Our dead are buried from our eyes,
We gather what is left.

The books they loved, the songs they sang,
The little flute whose music rang,
So cheerily of old,
The pictures we had watched them paint,
The last plucked flower, with odor faint,
That fell from fingers cold.

We smooth and fold with reverent care
The robes the living used to wear
And painful pulses stir
As over the relics of our dead,
With bitter rain of tears, we spread
Pale purple lavender.

And when we come in after years,
With only tender April tears
On cheeks once white with care,
To look on treasures put away
Despairing on that far off day,
A subtle scent is there.

Dew wet and fresh we gather them,
These fragrant flowers, now
every stem
Is bare of all its bloom.
Tears wet and sweet we strewed them here
To lend our relics, sacred, dear,
Their beautiful perfume.

The scent abides on book and lute,
On curl and flower, and with its mute
But eloquent appeal,
It wins from us a deeper sob
For our lost dead, a sharper throb
Than we are meant to feel.

It whispers of the "long ago,"
Its love, its loss, its aching woe,
And buried sorrows stir.
And tears like those we shed of old
Roll down our cheeks as we behold
Our faded lavender.

Julie Posey

I Gave My Boy to His Country

I gave my boy to his country
And he sailed away to sea.
I waved farewell to the boy I knew,
For his Captain had said to me,
"Even if death shall pass him through,
This Boy will never come back to you."

I gave my boy to his country
And he never came back to me
Though death had played for his life and lost.
Though his body and mind went free,
War touched his spirit with fire and frost,
A man had been born at an awful cost.

I gave my boy to his country
And it sent a man back to me.
My part of the price for the world's advance
His boyhood lost for liberty.
Death spared the man, by some glad chance.
But the boy that he was had died in France.

*That he would grant unto us, that we being
delivered out of the hand of our enemies might serve
him without fear, In holiness and righteousness
before him, all the days of our life.
Luke 1:74-75*

The Day God Took You Home

You never said you're leaving,
You never said goodbye,
You were gone before I knew it,
And only God knew why.

A million times I needed you,
A million times I cried.
If love alone could have saved you,
You never would have died.

In life I loved you dearly,
In death I love you still.
In my heart you hold a place,
That nobody could ever fill.

It broke my heart to lose you,
But you didn't go alone
For part of me went with you,
The day God took you home.

*God is our refuge and strength,
a very present help in trouble.
Psalm 46:1*

Julie Posey

It Is Not For Thee I Am Weeping

It is not for thee I am weeping,
It is not for thee my tears flow,
Thou canst not, thou canst not be sleeping
With earth for thy pillow— Ah no.

A loved one my heart fondly cherished,
An Angel all spotless has flown,
A flower in blooming has perished,
I feel, oh! I feel I'm alone.

But it is not for thee I am weeping,
It is not for thee my tears flow,
Thou canst not, thou canst not be sleeping
With earth for thy pillow— Ah no.

How I bitterly dread each tomorrow!
Even my dreams are of trouble and pain,
On my heart is the weight of deep sorrow,
And the night-cloud has set on my brain.

In this short, transient scene—this ideal,
This moment to what is to be,
I am missing a glorious real,
But it cannot, it cannot be thee.

Oh! it is not for thee I am weeping,
It is not for thee my tears flow,
Thou canst not, thou canst not be sleeping
With earth for thy pillow— Ah no.

As water in rock is imbedded,
Thou wert grown in the heart of my heart,
And we seemed so unchangeably wedded,
That nothing could tear us apart.

Thou wert mine, and I thine, and forever,
From each other we could not break free—
Could I live and without thee? Ah never!
What was life? What were hope without thee?

Oh! it is not for thee I am weeping,
It is not for thee my tears flow,
Thou canst not, thou canst not be sleeping
With earth for thy pillow. Ah no.

Every joy of this world, every pleasure
Has vanished before me and fled,
For they told me, thou all priceless treasure,
It was thou, it was thou who wert dead.

But each day and each night thou art before me,
And in visions thy sweet face I see,
And I rest with thy form bending o'er me,
Oh! It cannot—it cannot be thee.

Oh! It is not for thee I am weeping,
It is not for thee my tears flow,
Thou canst not, thou canst not be sleeping
With earth for thy pillow. Ah no.

Julie Posey

Why Do You Weep?

Oh child of grief, why do you weep now?
Why droops your sad and mournful brow?
Why is your look so like despair?
What deep, sad sorrow lingers there?

In all the varying scenes of woe,
The lot of fallen man below,
Still lift your tearful eye above,
And hope in God for God is love.

Sweet is the thought, time flies apace,
This earth is not our resting place;
And sweet the promise of the Lord,
To all who love his name and word.

Then, weeping pilgrim, dry your tears,
Comfort on every side appears;
An eye beholds you from above,
The eye of God and God is love.

What time I am afraid, I will trust in thee.
Psalm 56:3

Julie Posey

Lines to a Young Mother

Young mother! What can feeble a friendship say,
To soothe the anguish of this mournful day?
They, they alone, whose hearts like yours have bled,
Know how the living sorrow for the dead.

Each tutored voice, that seeks such grief to cheer,
Strikes cold upon the weeping parent's ear.
I've felt it all, oh yes! Too well I know
How vain all earthly power to hush thy woe.

God cheer you, childless mother! It is not given,
For man to ward the blow that falls from heaven.
I've felt it all as you are feeling now.
Like you, with stricken heart and aching brow.

I've sat and watched by a dying beauty's bed,
And burning tears of hopeless anguish shed.
I've gazed upon the sweet, but pallid face,
And vainly tried some comfort there to trace.

I've listened to the short and struggling breath,
I've seen the cherub eye grow dim in death.
Like you, I've held my head in speechless gloom,
And laid my first born baby in the silent tomb.

*As one whom his mother comforteth, so will
I comfort you; and ye shall be comforted in Jerusalem.
Isaiah 66:13a*

In My Despair I Sit

While in my silent room I sit,
And muse with growing dread,
Upon the past and coming years,
Whence every hope has fled.

I feel that it were best to die,
And flee this world of grief,
Oh! Friend, in mercy pity me.
Oh! God, give me relief!

Oh! Give me Hope
Oh ! Give me Joy,
Lest grief, and woe,
my soul destroy.

*Peace I leave with you, my peace I give unto
you: not as the world giveth, give I unto you.
Let not your heart be troubled, neither let it be afraid.
John 14:27*

Julie Posey

Mother, What Is Death?

Mother, how still the baby lies,
I cannot hear his breath,
I cannot see his laughing eyes,
They tell me this is death.

My little work I thought to bring,
And sat down by his bed,
And pleasantly I tried to sing,
They hushed me-he is dead.

They say that he again will rise,
More beautiful than now,
That God will bless him in the skies.
"Oh, mother, tell me how!"

"Daughter, do you remember, dear,
The cold, dark thing you brought,
And laid upon the casement here,
A withered worm, you thought?"

I told you that almighty power
Could break that withered shell,
And show you, in a future hour,
Something would please you well.

"Look at the chrysalis, my love,
An empty shell it lies,
Now raise your wondering glance above,
To where yon insect flies!"
"Oh, yes, mamma! How very gay
Its wings of starry gold!
And see! it lightly flies away
Beyond my gentle hold.

Oh, mother, now I know full well,
If God that worm can change,
And draw it from this broken cell,
On golden wings to range.

How beautiful will brother be,
When God shall give him wings.
Above this dying world to flee
And live with heavenly
things!"

*Have not I commanded thee? Be strong
and of a good courage; be not afraid, neither
be thou dismayed: for the LORD thy God is
withy thee whithersoever thou goest.
Joshua 1:9*

Julie Posey

Pearls of Beauty

It is said that when the mollusk
Hides within its narrow shell,

Bits of sand or tiny pebbles
Which it cannot forth expel,

That it shrinks not from the chafing,
Nor laments its presence there.

But at once begins to form them
Into pearls of beauty rare.

She Died in Beauty

She died in beauty, like a rose blown from its parent stem.
She died in beauty, like a pearl dropped from some diadem.

She died in beauty, like a lay along a moonlit lake.
She died in beauty, like the song of birds amid the brake.

She died in beauty, like the snow on flowers, dissolved away.
She died in beauty, like a star lost on the brow of day.

She lives in glory, like night's gems set round the silver moon.
She lives in glory, like the sun amid the blue of June.

For his anger endureth but a moment;
in his favour is life: weeping may endure
for a night, but joy cometh in the morning.
Psalm 30:5

Poems and Prayers for Grieving Parents

Tears

Flow, tears! You have a spell,
A gentle spell, which weaves
Itself over my sad heart,
And it dull woe relieves.

Ye are all eloquent,
In your soft, silent flow.
When, lone and musingly,
I feel my heart sink low.

Ye soothe the aching sense
Of pain, which pressing weighs
Upon the troubled soul,
And all its youth decays.

You are not for the gaze
Of the cold, scornful eye.
No mocking look shall rest,
None know, but purity.

And you shall mingle
With the dews of even
Soft pity may descend
And bear you up to heaven.

Hay tell how I have wept,
Have agonized alone,
While "rainbow tinted hopes,"
Have faded, one by one.

And, sadder far than all,
The burning anguish wrung

By sin, whose withering touch
Upon my spirit hung.

And left her taint accurse,
Grieving the holy dove,
Which fondly hovered there,
An earnest of God's love.

Flow, tears! flow on, and calm
This troubled, aching breast;
Your mournful tenderness
Lulls agony to rest.

Hope gushes with you,
Telling of that fair land
Where tears are wiped away
For aye, by God's own hand.

I will believe, and live.
The cross of Christ I take,
My God accepts my tears
For his dear Jesus' sake!

The Comfort of the Promises

Upon life's journey are you growing weary?
And by its burdens are you quite oppressed?
These words come softly over the pathway dreary,
"Come unto me, and I will give you rest."

Within your heart are strife and tumult raging?
Kneel down alone, in silent, trustful prayer;
And when you touch the hand of the Eternal,
" The peace of God" shall rest upon you there.

Are darkness and thick clouds above, around you?
Obscuring every blessing from your sight?
Again there come sweet words, so full of comfort,
He says, "At eventide it shall be light."

Do anxious cares drive from your eyelids slumber?
Know that this promise He will surely keep.
Rest in sweet peace; be this your consolation,
" For so He gives His beloved sleep."

And of the future do grave doubts assail you?
And do you fear to breast the final tide?
Sweetest of all, these words come softly stealing,
"When I awake with Thee, I shall be satisfied."

This is my comfort in my affliction: for thy word hath quickened me.
Psalm 119:50

Julie Posey

The Bottom Drawer

In the best chamber of the house,
Shut up in dim, uncertain light,
There stood an antique chest of drawers,
Of foreign wood, with brasses bright.

One day a woman, frail and gray,
Stepped totteringly across the floor,
"Let in," said she, "The light of day,
Then, Jean, unlock the bottom drawer."

The girl, in all her youth's loveliness,
Knelt down with eager, curious face.
Perchance she dreamed of Indian silks,
Of jewels, and of rare old lace.

But when the summer sunshine fell
Upon the treasures hoarded there,
The tears rushed to her tender eyes,
Her heart was solemn as a prayer.

"Dear Grandma," she softly sighed,
Lifting a withered rose and palm.
But on the elder face was nothing
But sweet content and peaceful calm.

Leaning upon her cane, she gazed
Upon a baby's half worn shoe.
A little frock of finest lawn,
A hat with tiny bows of blue.

A ball made fifty years ago,
A little glove, a tasseled cap,
A half done "long division" sum,
Some school books fastened with a strap.

She touched them all with trembling lips,
"How much," she asked, "can the heart bear?"
Ah, Jean! I thought that I should die
The day that first I laid them there.

But now it seems so good to know
That through these weary, troubled years
Their hearts have been untouched by grief,
Their eyes have been unstained by tears.

Dear Jean, we see with clearer sight
When earthly love is almost over,
Those children await me in the skies,
For whom I locked that sacred drawer.

*Let your conversation be without covetousness;
and be content with such things as ye have: for he
hath said, I will never leave thee, nor forsake thee.
Hebrews 13:5*

Julie Posey

The Death of Infants

`When a portion of home's sunshine is withdrawn, when one of the merry voices that made sweet music for us is hushed forever, then we feel the worth of the treasure removed from our care; and the depth of our sorrow is proportioned to the intensity of our affection. "We miss the small step on the stair;"we miss the little arms that used to twine so lovingly around our neck, the soft cheek that pressed our own, the smiling lips that gave so sweet a good-night kiss; we see the favorite toys' laid carefully aside, the little chair unoccupied, the cradle and the crib untenanted; we can turn no way without meeting something to remind us of our loss. Those who have wept over the coffin in which rested the shrouded form of a little one, know well that this is so. They are gone from us; but they are not forgotten. Their names are treasured in our heart of hearts;- their love abides with us forever.

`There is often a solemn beauty impressed on the features of an infant, after the chill hand of Death has touched it. I remember, as if it were but yesterday, the hour when I first stood beside the coffin of a child, a little girl of four years old. There was a spiritual beauty on her face that I had never seen there before. The fair hair, parted smoothly over the pure, pale brow, the closed eyes, the round, dimpled cheek, the slightly parted lips, all bore the impress of the Destroyer; yet all were beautiful. It seemed as if the peace of the home her spirit had found was reflected on the frail dwelling it had left.

`The custom of placing flowers in the coffin of the little child, is, I think, beautifully appropriate. What fitter emblem could be found, than a delicate rose bud or a deep blue violet, of the brief existence of the cherished one transplanted from the desolate wilds of earth to the garden of heaven? Who could wish that frail bud again exposed to the blighting frosts of a cold, selfish world? Well might even the one whose warm heart's love had twined most closely around it, well might the mother of that little one have said,

> "Go to thy rest, my child!
> Go to thy dreamless bed,
> Gentle and undefiled,
> With blessings on your head.
> Fresh roses in thy hand,
> Buds on thy pillow laid,
> Haste from this fearful land
> Where flowers so quickly fade."

There is consolation in the midst of the bitter anguish attending such a bereavement. The fair brow that has been so carefully sheltered from the storm, will never be exposed to its violence. The young heart that answered so joyously to the accents of tender affection, 'will never thrill to the tones of, harshness, or sink beneath the pressure of sorrow. The little feet, that have been led so carefully along the smooth pathway of opening life, will never toil wearily up the steep ascent, or turn suddenly aside, to seek the path that leads to destruction. Nor is this all. Is it not a blessed source of consolation to a mourning parent's heart, to think, I have a babe in heaven? Is there not deep joy in the love, that, purified by sorrow, rises from earth to a holier sphere? Surely there is. And is there not sweet music in the words, "Suffer little children to come unto me, for of such is the kingdom of heaven?"

Julie Posey

The Last Kiss

There lies my dear one in her funeral dress,
A last smile lingering on these muted lips,
The eyes, once bright, are in a dark eclipse,
Her cold cheek answers not to my caress.

This is a woe beyond all might to bless.
Now, my strayed child from another cup sips.
Or, maybe, in that River now she dips
For a first draught of still forgetfulness.

What shall I do, who would not have you die?
This grief is at the heart, and not for tears.
Upon my face the mask must soon be set.
I have come in to say a last good-bye,
To arm me for the period of lonely years.
Sweet, take my pledge that I shall not forget.

*For the LORD will not cast off for ever:
But though he cause grief, yet will he have
compassion according to the multitude of his
mercies. or he doth not afflict willingly
nor grieve the children of men.
Lamentations 3:31-33*

Julie Posey

The Star and the Child

A maiden walked at eventide
Beside a clear and placid stream,
And smiled, as in its depths she saw
A trembling star's reflected beam.

She smiled until the beam was lost,
As across the sky a cloud was driven;
And then she sighed, and then forgot
The star was shining still in heaven.

A mother sat beside life's stream,
Watching a dying child at dawn,
And smiled, as in its eye she saw
A hope that it might still live on.

She smiled until the eyelids closed,
But watched for breath until the even,
And then she wept, and then forgot
The child was living still in heaven.

Blessed are ye that hunger now: for ye shall be filled.
Blessed are ye that weep now: for ye shall laugh.
Luke 6:21

The Tear of Sympathy

How softly the tear of sympathy falls on the heart bruised and broken with sorrow! It assures the sad and weeping soul that it is not alone in a wilderness of cold hearts and that there are those who can feel for the troubles of others. What is more cheering to an aching heart than such a thought? The desire to be loved is human nature in its purity. It is the first impulse of the opening heart and it lives and breathes inside of us all until the hour of death. A look of love, a word of kindness, a tear of sympathy, costs us nothing. Why, then, withhold them from those who would prize them as blessings winged with the fragrant dews of heaven? To give them, costs nothing; but it often costs us an effort. A silent pang at the heart, did we but confess it. To withhold them, for he must indeed be full of hatred and whose heart does not delight in going forth to bless and be blessed.

The tear of sympathy never falls in vain. It waters and fertilizes the soil of the most sterile heart, and causes it to flourish with the beautiful flowers of gratitude and love. And as the summer clouds weep refreshment on the parched earth, and leave the skies more beautiful than before, with the rainbow of promise arching in the cerulean dome; so the tear of sympathy not only refreshes the heart on which it drops, but it elevates and beautifies the nature of him from whom it springs. A sympathizing heart is a spring of pure water bursting forth from the mountain-side. Ever pure and sweet itself, it carries gladness and joy on every ripple of its sparkling current.

They that sow in tears shall reap in joy.
Psalm 126:5

Julie Posey

Thinking

If you think you are beaten, you are.
If you think you dare not, you don't.
If you'd like to win but you think you can't,
It's almost a cinch you won't.

If you think you'll lose, you're lost,
For out of the world we find
Success begins with a fellow's will,
It's all in the state of mind.

If you think you're outclassed, you are.
You've got to think high to rise,
You've got to be sure of yourself before
You can ever win a prize.

Life's battle doesn't always go
To stronger or faster men,
But sooner or later the man who wins,
Is the one who thinks he can.

*But whoso hearkeneth unto me shall dwell
safely, and shall be quiet from fear of evil.
Proverbs 1:33*

Weep Not For Her

Weep not for her, there is no cause for woe,
She died before the heart had learned to sin,
Before the cheek had lost its summer glow,
Or winter chilled the monitor within,

The fairest flowers of earth do quickly fade,
Ever sorrow's cruel hand is on them laid -
Weep not for her.

*In every thing give thanks: for this is the
willof God in Christ Jesus concerning you.
1 Thessalonians 5:18*

Julie Posey

To a Bereaved Mother

Sure, to the mansions of the blessed
When infant innocence ascends,
Some angel, brighter than the rest,
The spotless spirit's flight attends.

On wings of ecstasy they rise,
Beyond where worlds material roll,
Till some fair sister of the skies
Receives the unpolluted soul.

That inextinguishable beam,
With dust united at our birth,
Sheds a more dim, discolored gleam
The more it lingers upon earth.

Closed in this dark abode of clay,
The stream of glory faintly burns,
Not unobserved, the lucid ray
To its own native fount returns.

But when the Lord of mortal breath
Decrees his bounty to resume,
And points the silent shaft of death
Which speeds an infant to the tomb.

No passion fierce, nor low desire,
Has quenched the radiance of the flame,
Back to its God the living fire
Reverts, unclouded as it came.

Fond mourner, be that solace thine!
Let Hope her healing charm impart,
And soothe, with melodies divine,
The anguish of a mother's heart.

Oh, think! The darlings of thy love,
Divested of this earthly clod,
Amid unnumbered saints above,
Bask in the bosom of their God.

Of their short pilgrimage on earth
Still tender images remain,
Still, still they bless thee for their birth,
Still filial gratitude retain.

Each anxious care, each rending sigh,
That wrung for them the parent's breast,
Dwells on remembrance in the sky,
Amid the raptures of the blessed.

Over thee, with looks of love, they bend;
For you the Lord of life implore,
And often from sainted bliss descend,
Thy wounded quiet to restore.

Often, in the stillness of the night,
They smooth the pillow of your bed,
Often, till the morn's returning light,
Still watchful hover over your head.

Hark! in such strains as saints employ,
They whisper to you bosom peace.
Calm the perturbed heart to joy,
And bid the streaming sorrow cease.

Then dry, henceforth, the bitter tear:
Their part and yours inverted see,
You were their guardian angel here,
They guardian angels now to see.

We Will Laugh Again

We all know what Time can do even for the sharp pangs of a great bereavement. In the first dark and cloudy day it seems as though no light will ever fall upon our path again. I shall never laugh anymore." Oh, yes, you will!

Time, the Lord's ameliorative, will begin to minister to the broken spirit, and however incredible it may now appear, some day the smiles will come back in the blanched cheek, and the mouth will be filled with laughter. Let us never forget when we are counting our blessings to thank God for the glorious ministry of time.

For he is our peace, who hath made
both one, and hath broken down
the middle wall of partition between us;
Ephesians 2:14

To an Infant in Heaven

Your bright and star like spirit!
That, in my visions wild,
I see, mid heaven's seraphic host
Oh! Can you be my child?

My grief is quenched in wonder,
And pride arrests my sighs.
A branch from this unworthy stock
Now blossoms in the skies.

Our hopes of you were lofty,
But have we cause to grieve?
Oh! Could our fondest, proudest wish
A nobler fate conceive?

The little weeper, tearless,
The sinner snatched from sin,
The babe, to more than manhood grown,
Before childhood did begin.

And I, your earthly teacher,
Would blush your powers to see,
Your are to me a parent now,
And I, a child to thee!

What bliss is born of sorrow!
'Tis never sent in vain,
The heavenly surgeon maims to save,
He gives no useless pain.

Our God, to call us homeward,
His only Son sent down,
And now still more to tempt our hearts
Has taken up our own.

Julie Posey

To Each His Own

Each has his drug for sorrow
(Or else the pain would slay!)
For one, it is "Tomorrow",
For one, it is "Yesterday."

And have you lost, my brother?
Yes, but in dreams I find.
"And I" (so says another)
"Leave buried dead behind!"

For each, when griefs are fretting,
A different balm must be.
Some find it in forgetting,
And some in memory.

Trust in the LORD with all thine heart; and lean not unto thine own understanding. In all thy ways acknowledge him, and he shall direct thy paths.
Proverbs 3:5-6

Julie Posey

To a Friend on the Loss of a Child

When on my ear your loss was knelled,
And tender sympathy upburst,
A little spring from memory welled
Which once had quenched my bitter thirst.

And I was fain to bear to you
A portion of its mild relief,
That it might be as cooling dew
To steal some fever from your grief.

After our child's untroubled breath
Up to the Father took its way,
And on our home the shade of death
Like a long twilight haunting lay,

And friends came round with us to weep
The little spirit's swift remove,
This story of the Alpine sheep
Was told to us by one we loved.

They in the valley's sheltering care,
Soon crop their meadow's tender prime,
 And when the sod grows brown and bare,
The shepherd strives to make them climb.

To any shelves of pasture green,
That hang along the mountain side,
Where grass and flowers together lean,
And down through mists the sunbeams glide.

But nought can lure the timid thing
The steep and rugged path to try,
Though sweet the shepherd call and sing,
And seared below the pastures lie.

Till in his arms their lambs he takes,
Along the dizzy verge to go,
When heedless of the rifts and breaks,
They follow on over rock and snow.

A blissful vision through the night
Would all my happy senses sway,
Of the Good Shepherd on the height,
Or climbing up the starry way,

Holding our little lamb asleep,
And like the burden of the sea
Sounded that voice along the deep,
Saying, "Arise, and follow me!"

I have seen his ways, and will heal him: I will lead him also, and restore comforts unto him and to his mourners.
Isaiah 57:18

Psalms of Comfort

Psalm 23
1 The LORD is my shepherd; I shall not want.
2 He maketh me to lie down in green pastures: he leadeth me beside the still waters.
3 He restoreth my soul: he leadeth me in the paths of righteousness for his name's sake.
4 Yea, though I walk through the valley of the shadow of death, I will fear no evil: for thou art with me; thy rod and thy staff they comfort me.
5 Thou preparest a table before me in the presence of mine enemies: thou anointest my head with oil; my cup runneth over.
6 Surely goodness and mercy shall follow me all the days of my life: and I will dwell in the house of the LORD forever.

Psalm 46
1 God is our refuge and strength, a very present help in trouble.
2 Therefore will not we fear, though the earth be removed, and though the mountains be carried into the midst of the sea;
3 Though the waters thereof roar and be troubled, though the mountains shake with the swelling thereof. Selah.
4 There is a river, the streams whereof shall make glad the city of God, the holy place of the tabernacles of the most High.
5 God is in the midst of her; she shall not be moved: God shall help her, and that right early.
6 The heathen raged, the kingdoms were moved: he uttered his voice, the earth melted.
7 The LORD of hosts is with us; the God of Jacob is our refuge. Selah.
8 Come, behold the works of the LORD, what desolations he hath made in the earth.
9 He maketh wars to cease unto the end of the earth; he breaketh the bow, and cutteth the spear in sunder; he burneth the chariot in the fire.
10 Be still, and know that I am God: I will be exalted among the heathen, I will be exalted in the earth.
11 The LORD of hosts is with us; the God of Jacob is our refuge. Selah.

Psalm 96

1 O sing unto the LORD a new song: sing unto the LORD, all the earth.
2 Sing unto the LORD, bless his name; shew forth his salvation from day to day.
3 Declare his glory among the heathen, his wonders among all people.
4 For the LORD is great, and greatly to be praised: he is to be feared above all gods.
5 For all the gods of the nations are idols: but the LORD made the heavens.
6 Honour and majesty are before him: strength and beauty are in his sanctuary.
7 Give unto the LORD, O ye kindreds of the people, give unto the LORD glory and strength.
8 Give unto the LORD the glory due unto his name: bring an offering, and come into his courts.
9 O worship the LORD in the beauty of holiness: fear before him, all the earth.
10 Say among the heathen that the LORD reigneth: the world also shall be established that it shall not be moved: he shall judge the people righteously.
11 Let the heavens rejoice, and let the earth be glad; let the sea roar, and the fulness thereof.
12 Let the field be joyful, and all that is therein: then shall all the trees of the wood rejoice
13 Before the LORD: for he cometh, for he cometh to judge the earth: he shall judge the world with righteousness, and the people with his truth.

Made in the USA
San Bernardino, CA
30 August 2014